Milly and M Help the Animals

"We may look different
but we feel the same."

Milly and Molly know a special place,
where the houses thin out and the hills begin.

Where there are trees and streams and ponds.
A quiet place the animals call their home.

But all that changed one day when the developers moved in with their machines. "Help," cried the plovers.

"Don't let them flatten our nesting place
Where on earth would we go then?"

"Help," cried the hedgehogs.

"Don't let them remove our hedge.
Where on earth would we go then?"

"Help," cried the frogs.

"Don't let them drain our pond.
Where on earth would we go then?"

"Help," cried the field mice.

Don't let them mow our grass.
Where on earth would we go then?"

"Help," cried the rabbits.

"Don't let them pave our land.
Where on earth would we go then?"

"Help," cried the otters.

"Don't let them dam our stream.
Where on earth would we go then?"

"Help," cried the birds.

"Don't let them cut down our trees.
Where on earth would we go then?"

"We'll take care of this," said Milly and Molly.
"Where are the men who do these things?"

"There they are," cried the animals.

"We can't let you do these things. We can't stand by and watch," said Milly and Molly. The developers took off their hats and shuffled their feet.

"Where do we go, if we don't go here?" they asked.

"To a place where no animals live," said Milly and Molly.

Milly and Molly helped the men move the pegs and build a fence.

"This is a special place," they said.
"A quiet place the animals call their home."

Milly and Molly put up a sign.
"There," they said. "That takes care of that!"